I WISH SHE KNEW

I Wish She Knew

Lessons Learned on Life's Journey

Donna Davis
CEO

D W Davis Consulting, LLC

First Printing, 2021

CONTENTS

DEDICATION

I dedicate this book to my eighteen-year-old self. You were brave when you didn't know what bravery was. You overcame so much. You didn't let poverty, being bullied, or being a victim of domestic violence dictate the direction of your life.

You fought through the feelings of rejection, unworthiness, and poor self-image. You cried out to God in your distress and He heard your cries. All of your tears were precious in His sight. You are loved and your life matters.

INTRODUCTION

It is easy to brush feelings aside that make us feel uncomfortable. Feelings such as unworthiness and fear. We don't deal with them outwardly but they inwardly nag at our soul. They cause us to miss opportunities by shrinking back. Many incidents in my life had me doing exactly that. I realized that if I continued shrinking, one day I would be unrecognizable.

I did not want my future to be dictated by circumstances that I had no control over. It is not my fault that I grew up poor. I should never have felt embarrassed or ashamed of wearing the same clothes multiple days to school. Not having enough to eat was not the burden of a child. There is nothing wrong with wanting to be loved. I was not a mistake and the mistakes I made should not define my future.

Those were some lessons I learned. The journey to learning those lessons was not easy. There were times when I wanted to give up. I didn't. I always had a fire burning deep within me. When my fire was doused with bullying, loneliness and domestic violence, I did not give up. I don't know why I didn't give up.

One day the Spirit of God spoke to me. It was then that I realized why I kept fighting. God had created me for peace, for victory, and to be whole. The fire was extinguished, but an ember remained. When the Spirit of God and that ember collided, an eternal fire ignited within me. It was then that I knew that God kept me. God protected me. God loved me.

Throughout my life God was waiting on me. I am so glad I didn't give up on myself. I am so glad He waited.

1

1

BATTLE SCARS

Battle scars are not always seen, but they are a reminder that we have survived obstacles in our lives. Battle scars are a testament that we may have been broken, but broken people can be healed-not just physically, but emotionally and spiritually as well. The scars left behind have unbelievable stories they can tell.

The battle scars from abuse can be enormous. They can lead to fear, lack of trust and low self-esteem. We can relive the trauma of the abuse so much that we actually don't allow the wounds, the cuts, the shame to create a scab or scar tissue. We keep our trauma exposed to the elements so that anything that brushes up against them, adds to their pain and justify their exposure. It is easy in those instances to say things like:

"See, I can't trust anyone,

Look how they treat me or

it's my fault, I brought this on myself".

On our body, before a scar is formed, scabs sometimes come first.

I would implore you to not pick the physical or emotional scab. Overtime, they decrease in size and fall off as new skin and renewed emotions are formed.

I have dealt with many scabs that I didn't allow to turn into scars. One of those scabs was trust after my domestically violent marriage. My abuser started out unsuspecting and sweet, and he showered me with gifts and kind words until he had me where he wanted me. That's when the abuse happened. So every time a guy was nice, I suspected he was up to something and I was not going to become a victim again. Anyone after him was placed in the non-trust category because I ripped the scab off every time.

So how do you stop the cycle of:

healing-bleeding-healing-bleeding?

When you are wounded emotionally, know that it is okay to take time to heal. How much time? As much as you need. The healing process for me may actually be longer than the healing process for you. We're not competing for who can get over trauma the quickest; we all want peace.

As long as we are going through a process to acknowledge, confront, and release the emotional burden we have concerning our trauma and have not stalled in the midst of the pain by using protective barriers like anger, bitterness or unforgiveness, we are progressing. Discover things that can help you be healed, whole and complete.

So keep moving, keep believing that you can be more than a survivor; you can be an overcomer. Believe that emotions like past shame do not have to dictate your future actions.

-

It is okay to take time to heal.

2

THE BEGINNING

Summertime was the best time of the year when I was in elementary school. I spent countless hours playing outside with my sisters and by myself. We drew and played hopscotch and tic tac toe in the sand. Hide and seek, dodgeball, tag, and racing each other from one point to the next created some great memories.

I remember sneaking to pick blackberries because my dad thought we would get bitten by a snake, so he forbade us to pick them. Believe me, we were careful, but we could not resist the sweet blackberries that grew in abundance on the edge of our dirt road. We played outside with such joy. One thing was for sure, we could not go back and forth from the house to the outside throughout the day; we were forbidden to come in the house unless it was absolutely necessary. That did not bother us and the water hose kept us hydrated. Playing outside with my sisters, making mud pie meals and pretending to cook for each other was a great way for me and my sisters to pass the time during those warm summer days. We would use old jar tops and other discarded items from the house to use as our pots and plates. During these times, our imaginations were able to grow and develop. We could be anyone we wanted to be and make whatever dish we wanted to make. We were in control of the narrative during playtime.

It was as if we didn't have a care in the world. When we made our way back in the house, we were exhausted and content.

It was during some of these delightful exiles that I would make up songs and sing to the trees. I would sing whatever was inside me. I can only remember two words to one of the songs to this day. The song has somehow remained a part of my memory as something wonderful about my childhood. The song was called "Daddy's Girl" and those are the only words I can remember to the song. I would belt out those words and the trees would listen. I imagined myself standing before tons of people and I thought I had great vocal cords because I sang in the church choir and my dad sang in his own quartet group. It was only later in life that I discovered I did not inherit my dad's soulful tone in music, but his vocal ability translated into vocal speech for me.

As I reflect, it was while singing and making up songs in our dirt yard, that I knew I was creative and inventive and I didn't have to mimic anyone else to be accepted or successful. Even though I didn't have the exact gift of my parents, my gifts were making room for me as I commanded the attention of the trees as I pretended they were a captive audience wanting to hear more. I was demonstrating the ability to walk in my uniqueness and that the only thing I needed was what I already possessed.

Even though my vocal abilities did not sound that great to many people, it gave me comfort. It felt like I was being hugged with every vibration. The comforting embrace of my own voice-my own song caused me to keep singing into adulthood. When I needed peace, I would just sing whatever came out of my mouth, whatever I felt at the moment.

Somehow those imaginary meals guided me throughout my life. I had no idea what my life's purpose was, but I could tell if I wasn't doing it because I would not be satisfied and would search for something more. I was searching for the person I created as I pretended to cook mud pies. She was confident, she was skillful, she made the decisions and she was doing what she was created to do. I wanted to be her, not knowing I already was her. Somewhere along the journey of transforming into her, life got in the way. Circumstances and convenience caused me to settle and I may have still been in one of those many settled positions if the little girl that made up songs or created astounding mud pies didn't occasionally pop up and ask, "What about her?"

She was still there, just in a more mature body and she still wanted her dreams and desires to come true. I am so glad I didn't continue to brush her aside, but I looked for ways to validate her so she could exist.

Some of those circumstances that led me to settle weren't because I thought I couldn't achieve more or do better; some of it was because I felt inadequate, invisible and marginalized.

I don't recall any boy showing interest in me while I was in school. I had my childhood crush, but no one appeared to crush back. That is probably why in tenth grade when an older man showed interest in me, I fell for him. I jumped at the opportunity to be considered by someone and to be shown attention. Even later, after marrying him, that attention became negative. No one ever told me it was okay to not have a boyfriend and wait until it was right. The trajectory of my life changed from what I thought it would be even though it appeared to be coming true through the eyes of the little girl making mud pies in her yard. Even though things took a volatile turn, the little girl making mud pies and singing to the trees was still there, not wanting to settle. It was too late for her not to become a

statistic of poverty and so much more, but she could become a statistic that proves that your past and your circumstances can be overcome. I grew up in poverty, but I never thought that I could not triumph over those
circumstances.

3

PLAY WITH ME, PLEASE

Imagine being on the playground and everyone is having fun. They are laughing and whispering together. Everyone is engaged with at least one other person. Everyone except you. I was born with strabismus, better known by school age kids as "Cross eyed." I still cringe today when I hear adults making fun of people for something they were born with, something I saw as a defect. I had to wear what kids call "Coke bottle eyeglasses", and that did not help my situation. I was constantly picked on and laughed at.

When children were picking people to play baseball or to be on any teams, I was always one of the last people chosen.

I was constantly being asked who I was looking at. I was so self-conscious about my eyes and how I appeared that I looked down or away when I was talking to someone. What made it even worse were the times when it was just me and one other person in the room and we would talk and they would still ask me if I was looking at them. I wanted to scream, "You're the only one in the room! I already know my eyes are pointed in different directions! I don't need you to remind me!" It was these constant encounters that caused me to cower away in rooms I should have felt comfortable standing tall in. I was

self-conscious and felt that I would never be good enough no matter what I did. It made me look down or look away when

I was talking to someone. As a child, I was devastated and as an adult—still devastated. This affected my confidence, it caused me to devalue myself and it followed me during my lifetime.

Because of this, I always wondered how I could have performed better when someone told me I'd done a good job.

No one wanted to talk to me. No one wanted to play with me. What is an eight-year-old to do? I felt left out and accepted the fact that I was broken, something was wrong with me, I was too different and I would never be good enough.

Feeling that way became my norm and it solidified one day as I was lining up at the end of the school day to go home. I dropped my pencil on the floor. I bent down to pick it up, looking for it among the many legs blocking my view. Then, out of nowhere, it happened. Someone pushed me, and my head banged against the steel foot of a desk. As I grabbed my head, the bell rang and everyone went rushing out to catch the bus. No one looked back to help me. I was left looking at what appeared to an eight-year-old as a lot of blood in my hand from my head. My concern was getting to the bus so it wouldn't leave me, but my teacher took me to the nurse. The nurse put a big white gauze pad over my forehead. In my mind, I had already looked bad and was not beautiful to myself because of my crossed eyes and a scar that was over my right eye. With that gauze pad, I looked so much worse. I was crying. Not from the growing knot on my forehead, but because I knew that no one at home had a way to come get me once I had missed the bus. The nurse knew my family and didn't live too far from me, so she took me home.

I wish I had known then that I was valuable and had a lot to offer. I wish when I looked at everyone on the playground I could recognize that we all looked different. Differences don't make one person pretty and another ugly. Different makes each of us unique and there is value in uniqueness.

I struggled not only in elementary school but throughout my grade school. Actually, those feelings lasted more than twenty years after I graduated from high school.

I never felt confident in any setting because of my eyes.

I was left feeling that I was not good enough. The popular kids didn't want me to be a part of their group and even though I was somewhat smart—I was cross eyed. I was desperate to belong. I did whatever I could to be accepted.

I was smart in school. Consistently on the honor roll and racking up many academic accolades along the way. My grades were something I could control, but I never thought I was good enough. I wanted approval and acceptance, but I never had a best friend during my entire K-12 experience. I wasn't invited to birthday parties, sleepovers or just to hang out. I spent a lot of time feeling like I had to please people in order to fit in. The more I tried to please them, the more they required. That is a process that repeated itself into adulthood until I learned that the only person not being pleased in those situations was me. The people that I was trying to impress, subconsciously trying to get to be my friends, were not worth the energy, yet I poured it out until there was barely anything left for me.

I wanted others to value my intelligence and loyalty and my sense of humor, so I kept pouring myself out in every arena. I displayed fire only to discover that I was surrounded by water. As a college student, college graduate, promotion after promotion, master's degree,.....all of my accomplishments were hampered by low self-esteem because of my eyes. I always thought people were looking at me, judging me and not choosing me. I was the most knowledgeable person in some rooms I entered, and I felt like I didn't belong. I didn't look right so I didn't appear confident, and I found myself apologizing for having an opinion.

When I was forty-six, a friend that knew how self-conscious I was about my eyes told me about an eye doctor that performed surgery to correct strabismus. I had tried things over the years to try to straighten my eyes. I remember covering one eye to try to get the other eye to look straight, but my attempts at home remedies never worked. When I heard that someone could correct what was so visibly flawed about me, I was overwhelmed with joy and I jumped at the opportunity to not be judged, to look normal, to straighten my eyes.

The doctor told me about all of the risks, and they were not minor. He said that I could suffer from double vision if the calculations were not correct and the only way to fix double vision was to do surgery again. I don't think I fully listened to him. I wanted something I never had, my eyes straight and if it meant double vision, possible loss of vision, I was willing to take the risk. It was embedded in my soul that I needed fixing. I scheduled and went through with my surgery. I was scared on the day of the surgery. What if I couldn't see? What if the measurements were off and I had to go through surgery again? I swallowed hard and had these thoughts as the anesthesia set in.

I had to wear shades for a while after the surgery because my eyes were bloodshot. I did experience double vision for longer than expected and I began to fear that I had made a huge mistake, but eventually, the double vision went away.

Even with blood shot eyes, I looked in the mirror and was amazed that for the first time, my eyes were straight. No one would ever have to ask me again if I was looking at them. As my eyes cleared up and I could stop wearing the shades, I was excited to see the response of those around me. I would walk into rooms expecting people to immediately notice my straight eyes, but room after room, no one noticed. I resorted to asking people if they noticed anything different about me. Some people then noticed, most didn't. I had to point out to them that my eyes were now straight, and they would then realize it. Many people told me that they didn't pay attention to my eyes before.

Here I was, emotionally tortured to the point of risking blindness to look normal and to be accepted. I thought my crossed eyes jumped to the forefront in every situation I was in. That no one paid attention to what I was saying because of how I looked and here I was, fixed and I had to point it out to people.

I had surgery to correct my eyes, to correct my confidence, to correct my value only to discover that my confidence and value were never confined to a physical attribute that I was born with.

I wish the younger and older version of me knew that she was perfect just the way she was. That her eyes were a part of her uniqueness, her swag and her being because getting my eyes fixed did not fix my self-esteem or any of the negative things I thought about myself. Having the surgery actually helped me to realize that there was never anything wrong with me to begin with.

How many opportunities did I not take advantage of because I thought I was not enough? I was using someone else's mirror to determine my worth, to determine my view of myself.

That experience made me rethink other areas of my life that made me feel inadequate. I realized that I am more than flesh tone, hair, or a clothes size. I am fearfully and wonderfully made. I was created for purpose. I had dreams and desires that had been waiting on me to believe in me.

I came to the realization that if I say, I can't get it right or I always fail: guess what, I have what I speak. If I say I always fail, failure will be attracted to me and if I happen to achieve victory, I don't accept it: I say it was a fluke, that will never happen again and I further program my soul to be against me. My soul begins to think that it let me down because it let victory happen.

-

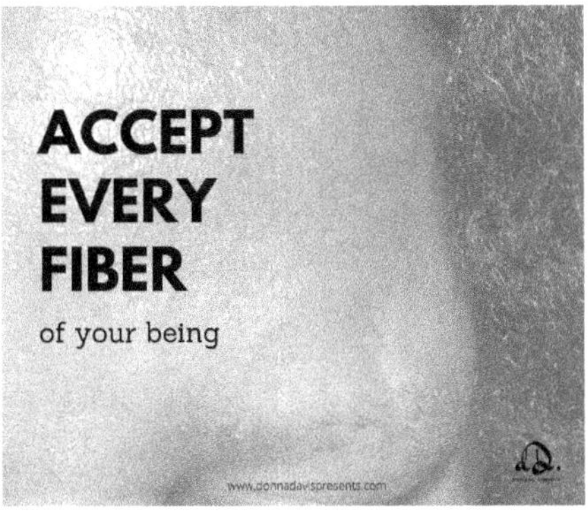

You see the scar above my right eye. For my entire life, I looked at it as something to prove that I wasn't worthy, that I wasn't beautiful. I let it hinder me from smiling at myself in the mirror, from accepting me.

I thought that others were judging me and I didn't blame them, I agreed with them. It only added to the other issues I had with me.

When I emotionally transformed from all the bad things that had happened to me and I brought along on my journey of life, It was then that I understood what this scar really meant.

It is a testament to everything I have overcome. It witnessed the poverty, the many nights I went to bed hungry, the bullying I endured in school, the rejection, the hate, the physical and mental domestic violence I overcame.

All of the odds I faced in life; this scar was there. It survived and when I look at it now, I see it as a badge of honor, as something that represents my true beauty, my strength to overcome. It sat quietly resting above my eye quietly yet screaming, that if I can heal from it, I can heal from anything.

I not only accept the good things about myself or the things that others point out, but I accept every fiber of my being, because I am a total package, not bits and pieces that someone can decide what parts they want.

I apologize to me, for the many years I did not accept myself. As I write this, the tears flow and there is so much beauty and growth in every drop.

4

BREATHE

The memories of playing make believe always bring a smile to my face. I looked forward to spending summer breaks with my aunt and her family in Summerville. My sisters and I were at our aunt's house when we found out our mom was having twins. I was eleven when my baby brother and sister were born. We went from a family of five to a family of seven and it was wonderful.

One morning; less than two months after the babies were born, I awoke to my mother screaming. My dad came running. My sisters and I were scared as we discovered that our baby brother had stopped breathing. My dad was trying to save him. We didn't have a phone or a hospital nearby, so we gathered up the babies and got my brother to help as quickly as possible. The people that worked on him tried for a long time to save him but it was too late.

In the following days, we had many people coming and going from our house. Everyone was sad. We had my brother, Daniel White Jr.'s memorial service at the grave site. I remember being there and feeling numb. Shortly after his service, people stopped coming to check on us. Sometimes when people stop coming, you wish that they continue for just a while longer.

We were told that my brother succumbed to Sudden Infant Death Syndrome (SIDS). The explanation was he got too comfortable while sleeping and forgot to breathe. Because he was a twin, we were told we had to watch my baby sister as she slept so we could shake her if she forgot to breathe. Watching my sister's chest go up, down, up, down is how I spent the remainder of my summer. I watched her in rotation with my parents and sisters. The moments when her chest stopped rising were scary, but we made sure that she breathed.

5

A DREAM

I met him when I was 16 and he was 23. No male had ever paid me any attention so when he did, I was excited. He asked permission to date me, and I thought that the dreams I always had were about to come true.

As a child, I had a recurring dream of being on a train that was about to wreck into a mountain and a tall male dressed in white would come and rescue me at the last minute. I always thought the dream gave me a vision of me being rescued out of poverty by my future husband.

He told me I had beautiful eyes. He called my crossed eyes beautiful and I felt that the love note I wrote in elementary school had finally been returned with a response.

I remember it so clearly. I had actually seen two boys in class that I liked. One day on the way home on the bus, I wrote each of them a note with a question. I asked them if they loved me and drew a box for yes and a box for no. I was trying to decide which one of them to give the note to first. I figured that at least one of them would say he loved me. Even then I was developing back up plans. In class the next day, I placed the note on the desk of one of the boys and the teacher saw me. She took the note and read it aloud to the class. I was embarrassed. I felt like my world was coming apart. There I was sitting at my desk surrounded by classmates that were laughing at me. The boy never mentioned the note to me. I got rid of the second note. I never wrote a note to another boy in elementary, middle or high school.

So here I was sitting in this person's car and he's telling me how he had been noticing me and wanted to date me. I was a sophomore in high school and he had come to my house. When I started spending time with him, I felt my childhood dreams were coming true. He took me places I had never been and bought me things I had never had. I had never been to a beautician, and he made sure my hair was done and that I didn't want anything. There were no raised voices or pressures to do anything I didn't want to do. At least that was my viewpoint at the time.

I got into an argument at home about spending time with him, so one day I left home and never returned. I went to a friend's house and called my boyfriend. I told him that I couldn't go back home, and he came and got me. He did not want me to stay with him because we were not married, so I stayed with one of his neighbors who could take me to school and bring me back home in the afternoons. She took care of me making sure I knew where to meet her in the afternoons and watching out for me like I was her daughter.

Eventually, my boyfriend said we would get married. Not the way that an 18-year-old still in high school envisioned being proposed to. He came and got me one afternoon. I wore a red sweater dress as he drove to a local pastor's house. We were married in the pastor's living room. No smiles, no celebration and no congratulations. Just a robotic process.

We then began living together and things went south fast. This person who had always shown me what I thought was love became controlling and abusive. He convinced me that my family didn't want anything to do with me, and he and his family were all I had. I was stuck and felt like I could never dig myself out of the situation I found myself in.

One saving grace was that I had been accepted into college. Because my husband cared about what other people thought, he did not want to keep me from attending college. I could not wait until the time came for me to go away. I would be living on campus. A reprieve from the verbal and physical abuse I experienced. The downside was that summer always came, and I had to go back to a domestic violence situation that remained constant.

My husband dropped me off at a hotel miles from Clemson. He did this more than a week before school began. That was convenient for him. I had to figure out how to get to campus on my own. I was scared and relieved at the same time. I was alone in a new city but I was no longer being abused. I eventually called my aunt to explain my situation. She and her son drove more than three and a half hours from Summerville to get me from the hotel. They took me to school when it was time.

After I graduated from college, there were no more reprieves. I lived my life trying not to anger my husband. He never seemed happy with me. Going to work became an escape. I had to walk a little over a mile at 4:30 am to ride a bus for more than two hours to get to my job on Hilton Head Island. The bus pulled up at our stop after 7:00 pm in the evening. I had to walk the distance back home.

One evening I was taken aback. When the bus pulled up to my stop so that I could make the mile trek home, my husband was there in the car to pick me up. He had never picked me up before. I was so happy that after being on my feet all day I could have a ride home. I got in the car and we took off. He was silent as we started down the road. I wasn't thinking about anything except how grateful I was to not have to walk home.

Then something happened that had me puzzled. He drove past our turn. I didn't say a word, but I was confused and thought that maybe we were going to the store. He said nothing. Like he knew our destination and had it planned. I remained quiet. I was growing more and more uneasy. Then he turned down a dirt road. I had never been down that road before. It was covered on both sides by towering cornfields that you could barely see above without straining your neck. He still said nothing. The further he drove, the more terrified I became. He kept driving and driving. I could no longer see the main road. I knew this couldn't be good and in the middle of my inward panic, he turned the car around. I thought we were going to head out, but he stopped the car. He put the car in park and spoke for the first time on our journey. He told me to get out of the car. I looked at him, and I was frozen with fear. I refused to get out and told him that I wasn't going to. He repeated his demand that I get out of the car, and he became angry as I continued to refuse. He grabbed his door handle and jumped out of the car.

He came around to the passenger side and snatched the door open. I was so frantic by this point that I had not thought about locking my door. He yelled at me to get out again and as I continued to refuse, he grabbed me by the arm and began pulling me out of the car. I tried to hold on to every part of the car I could to no avail. He yanked me out, and I landed on the ground. He began hitting me and kicking me with all of his strength.

I just knew that he was going to kill me. Right there in the road as I was screaming at the top of my lungs. We were so far down that dirt road that no one could hear me and in those moments I thought no one would even miss me. He spent our entire marriage convincing me that my parents, family and limited friends did not care about me. He kept me from them and he reminded me that they never called me, never checked on me, so they didn't love me and I believed him. Would anyone ever find my body if he just left me there to die?

As every hit and kick came, I realized that I didn't want to die. I didn't deserve to die, but I might die. My self-esteem was just as battered as my body, but there was an ember left that was gasping for air so that the fire to fight could ignite. In those horrible moments on the ground, being discarded, I remembered the fire I had to overcome poverty. I found myself, on that ground, in a situation that I wanted to overcome. I didn't want to die. I didn't want the final words I heard to be that of an abuser. I knew, while being beaten, that I was created for more. Not because I had ever experienced more. I knew that despite how I came into this world, despite all the obstacles I had faced to this moment, that I was made for more. I was worthy of more even though I was feeling only pain. I just needed to survive.

I don't know how much time passed. It seemed like an eternity. The hits kept coming and suddenly they stopped. I think he just got tired. He stood over me cowering in the fetal position on the ground and told me to get back into the car. I didn't move. I was crying uncontrollably covered in dirt mixed with tears. I told him that I wasn't getting into the car. He couldn't believe it. He had beaten me, making sure not to injure my face so no one would know of the abuse and there I was, a dejected pile on the ground and still my spirit wasn't broken. I was not showing total fear even though I was terrified of what each new moment would bring.

He picked me up and threw me back into the car. He got in, cranked up the car and drove home. I was in so much pain that I was just crying and shaking. At the house, I could hear him bragging to someone how he beat me and how I was screaming.

I then heard him laugh. I began to cry even harder and he came to where I was to tell me to be quiet. It was then that he told me the reason for my beating. I had embarrassed him in front of the neighbor and he needed to teach me a lesson.

It was at this point that I began apologizing to him. Of course, I had done something to cause him to lash out at me. In the midst of my tears and trembling, I kept telling him that I was sorry. He helped me to understand that it was my fault and that I needed to do better. Indeed, to stop thinking about a better life, I needed to accept my plight in life. Indeed to stop fighting the feeling of worthlessness and I needed to settle for being nothing. But the ember I felt trying to ignite down that dirt road would not let me discard me.

He never apologized for his actions. For beating me, kicking me or imbedding trauma in my soul. He felt he was justified. That he had set the order straight, and I had learned a lesson. I took that trembling with me even when I escaped his grips and filed for divorce. That fear and blow to my self-esteem followed me and guided decisions that I made until I realized that those negative emotions were controlling my life. I had to do something for my own well-being. As I was contemplating what to do, I remembered the ember that was in me that day as I lay on the ground, not knowing if I would ever get up. I remembered I told myself I was worthy even though I had lived a life not fully walking in value.

I realized that I needed to forgive him. Not because I was weak, not because I valued him more than I valued myself. He never thought he did anything wrong. He was wrong and I forgave him. I never told him I forgave him because the forgiveness I gave him was not for him. It was for me.

I forgave my abuser and he never asked. He thought it was his right to put me in my place, to make me fearfully submit. I don't even know if he ever felt any remorse or an ounce of regret.

I didn't report the abuse to the police, so he never faced the judicial system for anything he did to me and he should have. Forgiveness is an act of our will. It is a choice to release someone to God's judgement instead of our own. If I have a choice, and I do, I would prefer for God's judgement to be released on the person who has done me wrong instead of exacting justice myself. I have to trust God when I don't believe He is acting as fast as I want Him to when rendering judgement against someone who has harmed me.

If an abuser doesn't ask for forgiveness, what can we do? Usually, we hold it against the person. Sometimes for the rest of their lives. Hating them, praying that they suffer the same way we are suffering because of their words and actions against us or want them to suffer even more than we are.

When they do suffer, it could be from something unrelated to us, but we still think it's good because they deserve it. What happens is that we don't find ourselves feeling any better. Our eyes still fill with tears at the thought of what they did to us. We still have sleepless nights and suffer from trust issues and self-esteem issues because of our interaction with them. We will never forget, so how can we forgive? We don't have to forget, we shouldn't forget, and forgiving is not forgetting.

Forgiving is not condoning what has happened to us. Forgiving is allowing yourself to find a path forward out of the cloud of despair. We deserve to come to a place of peace even if what has happened to us left us in pieces.

I deserved better. I deserved to move on in spite of the pain and not be held hostage to what was done to me. I forgave him because I was worth having peace. I was worth being loved by myself. I owed it to myself to take my power back, and to be resilient in my soul. Not so I could endure more of the same from future relationships, but so I could never believe that I deserve to live my life by someone else's standard. My resilience wasn't rooted in anger; it was rooted in knowledge. Knowledge that I was made for more than being someone's punching bag, to make them feel like somebody while making me feel like nobody.

I was full of fire prior to meeting my ex-husband and I thought I could do anything. After marrying him and suffering I was reduced to ashes. The ember kept flickering, wanting oxygen, wanting to ignite again. If I didn't forgive him, I would not have gotten my fire back.

Forgiveness is for us because we don't deserve the physical, emotional or spiritual consequences of living in unforgiveness.

I had to evict the negative emotions that were not only formed that day, but the negative emotions that evolved from that day. It was worth moving forward without emotional bondage. It was worth living the life I was capable of living without negative emotions residing in my soul that didn't pay rent. I realized that he had moved on, remarried and never thought enough of me to give me closure from all of the abuse I suffered at his hands. He did not deserve to control my future with his past actions. I had to forgive him. Otherwise he would permeate every aspect of my life: how I interact with others, the goals I go after or cower from, and the relationships I became a part of. I decided he didn't deserve me, not only physically, but emotionally as well.

-

There was an ember left that was gasping for air.

6

A WAY OF ESCAPE

Being in an abusive relationship is hard to deal with physically, emotionally and in every aspect of life. When you fear getting yelled at, getting hit, getting dragged--it consumes your every move because your actions are for survival, to just exist. You don't tell anyone even though you want to, because it threatens your survival. You don't run away when you have an opportunity because you have nowhere to go.

You don't go to your family because you ran to the relationship to get away from them.

You don't run to your friends because they don't want to get involved.

You don't go to the church because your abuser is admired there or hold a position that you dare not cause a scandal.

Not only are you focusing on existing but not interfering or making others feel uncomfortable in their existence. How do you escape? How do you move on?

I felt trapped. I had graduated from college and had landed my first professional job as a teller for Wachovia bank.

I rode the bus to Hilton Head Island to get to work. The bus usually arrived about an hour before the bank opened. I couldn't stand up and wait outside the bank, so I would go to the McDonald's which was located a short distance away. I would go in and buy a coffee or a biscuit to justify sitting in there until the bank opened. I had decided that since it was so much time, I would read a book while I waited to make the most of my time.

The first book I chose changed my life. I was saved for about four years at this time. The majority of that time I had been in college. Now I was in the real working world, living full time with my abusive husband.

The book that I chose to read was **Good Morning Holy Spirit** by Benny Hinn.

As I read, I wept. Tears were streaming down my eyes so fast and hard that I had to go to the bathroom to hide in a stall. In that stall, I poured out every inch of tears that my body could create. I cried out to God and told Him that I wanted His Spirit to dwell in me. I believe I received the imparting of the Holy Spirit at that moment. I immediately knew that God did not create me to be physically or mentally abused and that I could not remain in that situation, but I still didn't know how to get out.

The scripture that I felt kept me bound because people who were more seasoned in their salvation shared it with me was: 1 Corinthians 7:13-14 KJV: 13.)*"And the woman which hath an husband that believed not, and if he be pleased to dwell with her, let her not leave him. 14.) For the unbelieving husband is sanctified by the wife, and the unbelieving wife is sanctified by the husband: else were your children unclean; but now are they holy."*

Verse 15a is what I looked to God to bring to pass.

"But if the unbelieving depart, let him depart."

I did not pay attention to 15b: " *A brother or sister is not under bondage in such cases: but God hath called us to peace."*

I didn't understand that part until much later. Be careful how you interpret scripture. If it is not coming directly from God, don't bind someone with your thoughts.

My problem was that he was fine abusing me, so in my undeveloped spiritual mind, I was trapped.

One thing I've learned about God: if your intentions are pure, He will meet you where you are until you get to where you need to be.

We lived with his mother and I knew he would never leave her, so I said one day to him (in her presence because the Holy Spirit had given me a boldness that even though I was afraid of getting knocked out, I said it anyway), "We need to get our own place." Everyone responded in shock, and he quickly said without skipping a beat, "You can find someplace, but I have a home."

God moved quickly. He met me where I was, and He gave me what I was looking for: a way out of an abusive marriage without getting beaten or dragged like I had been in the past. But, you guessed it, I didn't leave. Fear now converged on me. Where would I go (I had no long-term plan)? How would I make it? So when he told me I could go, I said nothing.

It's the response many abusers get when they dare their victims to leave or try to make it without them. I was isolated in my mind and I had no idea what to do, but I knew if I stayed, I would feel worthless and like a burden for the rest of my life.

A couple of days later, we were sitting in the living room. I know he and his mom had laughed at the fact that I had no one or nowhere to go, so I guess he decided to poke fun at me. He said, "Have you found a place yet?"

When he asked that, God dropped in my spirit that I needed confirmation from Him that my salvation was not tied to being abused. He knew my heart, and He gave me another opportunity to get it right. So I responded in faith. I said "Yes", I had found a place even though I hadn't. When I left that next morning, I went to work and got a hotel room that night. The following day I went to work and rode the bus back towards home that evening. I did not have enough money to continue staying in a hotel. I had called my sister the night before and she told me she would come get me and take me to Columbia where she lived.

When the bus stopped in the town on the way to where I lived, I got off and went to the payphone and called my cousin to see if she would come and pick me up. I told her I had left my abuser and needed her to come get me to take me to my mom's house. My cousin asked me where I was. I knew I was more than 20 miles from where she lived. I told her, and she told me to stay put because she was on her way. When she arrived, she asked me where my stuff was. I didn't even have a suitcase or plastic bag of clothes with me. Just what I had on my back. I told her all of my stuff was still at my abuser's house. My cousin told me to get in the car because we were going to get my stuff. Ya'll, I love her. As I reflect, it was as if we were snatching back from the enemy everything he tried to take from me.

I was crying and she told me as we pulled up in the yard that "I bet not let him see me cry." As we pulled up, my mother-in-law was placing black garbage bags of clothes and belongings on the back steps of the trailer. My cousin got out of the car with me, greeted my mother-in-law and asked me if that was my stuff. I said "Yes" and we started stuffing it all into her car. We went in to get the rest of my belongings and my cousin started pointing at items and asking me if they were mine. If I said yes, it went with us. If I said no, she left it alone. God was showing me that I always had people on my side. I just had to stop believing what my abuser was telling me. As we went through and gathered my belongings, I came to the point where I didn't want anything else even if it was mine.

My husband/abuser was sitting in the living room the entire time. He never got up. He never acknowledged that we were there. He just sat silently with his head turned in the opposite direction. All of a sudden, he didn't look menacing or abusive, but that's exactly who he was.

I got up enough courage to go to the living room and with his head still turned the entire time I was talking, I told him that I was sorry that it didn't work out. There I was, apologizing to someone who had beat me, dragged me, verbally assaulted my confidence, my existence. I knew it could have been a great marriage, but I knew I couldn't live for what it could be. I had to live for what actually was, so I left and never went back.

-

God did not create me to be physically or mentally abused.

7

MY DIVORCE EXPERIENCE

I grew up in an atmosphere where many couples who no longer got along would separate and remain married for years or decades. Some would even begin dating someone else or move in with someone else, but they would never sever the legal ties from their spouse. Maybe they considered it if they wanted to remarry, but usually they are content not having to make a marital commitment to someone else.

People would always say things like, " Child you should divorce him," but nobody really shared what that experience was like. How do you start? Where do you go?

When I left my ex-husband, my goal was either to reunite with him if counseling was successful or to divorce him. I made those choices, not because I had someone waiting in the wings, but because I deserved to be freed. Then when God blessed me with my Boaz, I would not still be legally attached to my past.

When I decided to get a divorce and researched the process in South Carolina, I thought that South Carolina only granted a divorce for three reasons, but it's actually five reasons:

1. Adultery
2. Habitual drunkenness or narcotics abuse
3. Physical cruelty
4. Desertion for a period of 1 year
5. One year's continuous separation (no-fault)

Unfortunately, I had several that I could choose from, but I did not want to have to go through proving his adultery by taking pictures of him at the hotel with his latest fling or deal with the emotional trauma of filing for physical cruelty and having to relive the trauma of being beaten. I could have chosen those, but I chose to file based on one year of continuous separation.

I kept track of our separation date and after a year had passed, I called him. We talked, and he discussed us getting back together. He was willing to take me back. No apology. No sign of regret. "I'll come get you." That was enough for him.

I wasn't opposed even after all of the abuse because I still loved him; however, during our one-year separation, I learned to love myself just as much as I loved him, if not more. And that is what changed the course of that conversation.

When he asked me to reunite, I said I would as long as we went to counseling. Being domestically abused should have been my non-negotiable, but it wasn't. I made my non-negotiable counseling (I still had so much growing to do.). I thought that if we went through counseling he would see the error of his ways. I thought counseling would reform him and he would never want to hit me again.

He said that he didn't need any counseling and I told him that I was filing for divorce. I chose me. Not my feelings, his feelings, his ego or sweet words. I chose me.

In choosing myself, I didn't know where to begin in the

divorce process. I wasn't going to let fear of the unknown hinder me from moving forward. Divorcing someone is a big deal, and there are many moving parts that I needed guidance on.

Something that stops people from filing for divorce is they can't afford a lawyer and I was no different. Lawyers were and are expensive, so I decided to represent myself. There is no law against representing yourself in a court of law, so I decided to do it. My issue then became that I needed divorce papers drawn up and I researched how to do it myself, but I thought better of it because I needed my filing papers to have all of the correct information.

In Columbia, we had this weekly paper called "The Penny Saver" where many businesses advertised. In the Penny Saver, I found an advertisement from a paralegal advertising that she would draw up divorce for a nominal fee. It was hard for me to afford, but I came up with it and hired her to draw up my divorce papers. When she completed them, I took them to the courthouse for filing and paid the filing fee.

It was then that I was informed that I had to serve my husband the divorce notice with the papers and date via certified receipt return. That should be simple enough right? It was not as simple as it should have been.

I sent the papers to my husband. A couple of weeks passed by and I never received the return receipt card. I got anxious because our hearing date was fast approaching and if I didn't have proof that I served him, I would have to start the process (including the filing fee) all over again.

Let me tell you: Obstacles are for conquering.

I went online to track the return card and discovered that it was returned to my post office, but it never left the post office to be delivered to me.

I did not have a car at this point in my life. I was desperate and asked a coworker if she would take me to the post office on our lunch break one day if I paid her. She took me to the post office and I explained to the clerk how desperately I needed that card. The person at the post office explained to me that they had misplaced the return receipt card and did not know where it was. They looked for it while I was there and came back and affirmed that it was lost.

I did not give up!!!

I reaffirmed the importance of that card in my divorce and I was told that they were sorry and that they would keep looking for it. I did not receive any comfort in those words.

On the way back to work, I was devastated and I tried to figure out my next move.

I got back to work and called the Better Business Bureau on my post office branch and filed a formal complaint.

Within an hour of filing my complaint, my postman called me and said "Mrs. Donna, I found your card. I had misfiled it earlier because I was off the day it was supposed to be delivered. You can come back and get it."

I explained that I didn't have a car and had paid someone to bring me to the post office on my lunch break. I could not come back, but he could bring it to me since it was his mistake. He didn't argue. He brought it to my job.

Now I had everything I needed to go to my divorce hearing.

Surely it would be smooth sailing from here on out.

Looking at my husband's signature on the return receipt card made the process more real. I didn't know if he was going to show up for the hearing or not, but I knew that I would be there. I had not changed my mind about representing myself, but I needed a witness to testify that I had actually been separated for more than a year. I struggled over who to ask. As I was sharing with a friend, he immediately said that he would be my witness. He had been supportive of me and whatever I wanted and he did not hesitate to help me end such a traumatic chapter in my life. He took off work to be there for me and he knows that I am grateful for his sacrifice and his friendship.

In the courtroom was the moment of truth. I was nervous, but I appeared confident. I was sweating and praying that no one could see the sweat. There I was, being my own lawyer with no experience. Unfortunately, I had only seen lawyers in the courtroom on TV. I knew the outline of how things would go. I would present my case and my husband would have the opportunity to present his case. My case only needed to consist of my witness testifying. I would then testify on my behalf that we had lived apart for one year. Also that we have irreconcilable differences that would prevent the marriage from being successful. This was clear cut enough, and I didn't see why the process couldn't be a simple divorce because:

1. We had no children, and
2. I didn't want anything from him.

I had never done anything like this before, but I knew that I was worth it. I understood I would stumble over my words, but as long as I kept going, it would be fine.

The defendant side of the courtroom was empty because my husband did not show up for the divorce proceedings.

I called my witness and had him swear to tell the truth and he testified that I had been separated for at least a year. Since my husband wasn't there nor had representation, my witness was not cross examined.

I then called myself to the stand and testified on my own behalf that we had been separated for at least a year and there was nothing that could be done to salvage the marriage. That was it. All I had to do was stop there and step down from the stand, but I had a little more to say.

In the initial divorce papers the paralegal drew up for me, she asked me several questions as she was writing them up. One of the questions she asked me was if I wanted my maiden name back. I said, "No."

As I was going through all of the obstacles that brought me to the courtroom, I realized that I had made a mistake with that decision. My confidence actually was building through every obstacle. I was saved at this point, and I knew that obstacles could be the hand of the enemy trying to keep me from what the Lord had in store for me. If the enemy was trying to discourage me so much in this process, what was the enemy trying to keep me from?

During the course of my testimony, I asked the court to reinstate my maiden name, and I knew the request was not in my paperwork. I requested my maiden name back because I did not want to give my father's legacy to someone who didn't deserve it. It was symbolic to me of being restored to who I was before the abuse was inflicted upon me.

I understood what my name meant, and I wasn't going to forever relinquish it with my divorce.

The judge, who had read my divorce decree, ruled that I had thirty days to amend my paperwork with the request of changing my last name back to my maiden name. I thanked him and he said, "Next time get a lawyer". I said nothing to him but thought to myself, "There won't be a next time".

It actually took me a while to track down the paralegal that drew up my divorce papers, but I found her and she amended them with no additional cost to me. I filed it timely and was granted my divorce.

It is one thing to divorce someone physically, it is something altogether different to divorce someone emotionally. All of the pain and trauma lingered with me long after the relationship ended. I developed trust issues. I was being held hostage by my emotions. Every time I tried to move forward, the guy would say something or do something that triggered my fears. I knew that if I didn't face the emotional baggage I had, I would never heal.

-

I learned to love myself.

8

EVOLVING

I eventually remarried. I have been married for more than twenty years. I was determined not to let the past cloud my vision of my future. I thought if I ignored the feelings or packed them away they wouldn't affect me. I spent many years trying to prove that I was worthy of acceptance and love. I didn't accept or love myself.

My husband and I thought long and hard about the things we wanted our children to experience. We were excited to begin parenthood. Twins run in my family and my husband's family. My grandmother and mother had twins so I should not have been surprised when the doctor told me that I was pregnant with twins. I thought that twins skipped generations but it did not skip any of ours. Fraternal twins were common in my family so I was sure we were having a boy and a girl.

Until the third month, my pregnancy was problem free. All of a sudden, I couldn't keep anything down. I was diagnosed with hyperemesis. I spent the remainder of my pregnancy in and out of the hospital. On one of these visits to the hospital my sister-in-law and I came up with names for the babies. We named them Ashley and Thaddeus.

At five months I had an ultrasound to check on the babies. The technician probed around my stomach and then we all heard swoosh, swoosh, swoosh. It was the heartbeat of one of our babies. I was beaming at the sound. When the technician went exploring for the second baby, her countenance changed. When I asked what was wrong she told me the doctor needed to come in. The doctor explained that one of the babies was no longer there and I had suffered what is called the vanishing twin syndrome. My son was the only baby there. For five months I looked forward to seeing Ashley and Thaddeus on the ultrasound. Somewhere in the process Ashley became our guardian angel.

Throughout my second marriage and raising my son anyone looking at me would have thought I had everything together. The truth is I had dealt with very little of the emotional trauma I had experienced prior to my second husband. I thought it was easier to push the feelings of inadequacy, worthlessness, fear and low self-esteem aside. They kept popping up. Those emotions told me to look down. They told me if I didn't please everyone, no one would care about me.

Over time I decided those emotions no longer defined me. I wanted to reclaim control over my life. I told those emotions I was done relinquishing my peace and self-worth to them. They had to go. It took time. I was worth the time. God remained with me the entire time.

I told those emotions
I was done
relinquishing my
peace and self-worth
to them.

2

I grew up in poverty. I was bullied in school. I overcame a domestically abusive marriage and other traumas. It took me many years but I learned how the emotions associated with my experiences have shaped my life and I want to share some of those lessons with you.

9

A MEASURE OF SUCCESS

On my journey to discover or walk in my purpose I can't let people cast their doubt cloud over my clear skies.

Being told that I can't do something should not cause me to shrink back, to cower in a corner or to give up before I have even begun.

If I tap into my purpose and walk in that direction, it will be more valuable than any amount of money or any materialistic thing could ever be.

I understand that my life experiences are not just random acts that have no connection to who I was meant to be. I realize that anything is possible.

Overcoming poverty, domestic violence, bullying, divorce and a whole host of other emotional traumas was not for me to give up and sit in a corner.

I understand in all those situations, heartaches, and despairs, that God had purpose for my life and I wasn't going to surrender to the pain, wallow in the pain or accept the pain when I knew that there was something beyond the pain. Without God, I could not see that there was even a way to move forward.

So when someone is laughing at your failures and your

attempts, and you have tears streaming down your face to the point that your eyes are burning and your lips are trembling, I need you to dig deep and try again. If not succeeding is the worst that could happen to you, then you are already ahead.

Not succeeding can only happen if you don't try. Did you try? Then you succeeded. We define success in the wrong ways sometimes. Success can be found not only in the results but in the attempts.

We all want success to the point that we don't realize when we have achieved a measure of success.

We receive a measure of success:

- Every time we try something new,
- Every time we study the moves of someone else to help us plan our next move,
- Every time we avoid a step because it didn't work out or help us the last few times we tried it.

Results may not be what we want and they may not need to be what we want, but they won't exist at all without attempts.

The First time I learned to play chess. I lost and may have been called a loser by the winner, even called unsuccessful. I actually played many games of chess in my life and have said "Checkmate" only a few times. Why do I keep playing if I keep losing? I learn a lot about how the game works in the process of playing. I get better with each attempt. Progression is winning.

-

Dig deep and try again.

10

MAKE TIME FOR YOUR DREAMS

I learned I have the ability to accomplish anything I want. It does not matter if I have wanted to do something for ten or fifteen years or since I was 6 years old.

I have been encouraging myself to move forward in fear. To become the person on the outside that I am on the inside.

There is no one else that can accomplish the things that I was created for. Life circumstances may have diverted me, but my dreams and goals are still waiting on me to focus on them.

I know you have spent so much time trying to help others achieve their goals that you didn't pay attention to the clock and now it appears a little late. You have poured into others, your children, your spouse, your parents, friends and coworkers. Now it's time to pour into you. To refill your cup because you have poured so much out that there is barely anything left for you. You are worth investing in you.

It may feel like you don't have time. You do.

What if you made a plan? What if you took small steps

towards your dreams? What if you just did it? You could fail of course, but one thing is certain, you would never succeed if you never try.

When I realized how much time I spent doing things like watching TV just to not remember half the stuff I saw, I began starting my day with the TV off and focusing at least 15-30 minutes minimum on accomplishing something towards a goal that I set for myself. It helped that I used a calendar to write out tasks to accomplish during the week towards my overall goals.

If we commit 4 to 5 straight hours to something, we may not accomplish what we set out to do. We may be so exhausted afterwards that it could be a long time before we work on our goal again.

If we chunk our time into 20-minute segments and use a calendar to track our plan, we can accomplish anything. Some of you may be saying, you'll never reach your goals at that rate. I promise, you will be closer to your goal than where you are right now.

Pour into yourself. Don't chastise yourself if you don't get something quite right; enough people already do that.

Give yourself grace.

Don't be afraid to make time for you. Replace that fear with purposeful steps to achieve what God has placed inside you.

There is no one else that can accomplish the things that I was created for.

11

DREAMS ARE AGELESS

I had dreams of what I wanted to be when I grew up. As I grew and focused on those desires I changed my mind as I learned more about myself and what I was truly passionate about. For the most part, I always held on to a portion of my original dream. Before I knew it, I had graduated from high school. I had entered a very unknown part of my life where I had to decide either to go into military service, community college, a four-year college or directly into the workforce. All great and viable choices. Life circumstances dictated so much in my life. One day I woke up and remembered what I wanted to be doing. I began taking steps in that direction.

Maybe your parents nurtured your dreams once you revealed it to them. Maybe they found programs and community events to involve you in so that your dream could be more etched into your being. Volunteer opportunities and mentors helped you to forge forward. Some of you are extremely happy with your outcome; others, not so much.

Maybe when you announced your lifelong dream at an age when you did not know what you chose, it was just what was popular at the time or something you saw on TV. Maybe someone caught you at a moment when you were playing with your toys and you had no idea that saying you wanted to be a doctor would turn your parents into super parents that involved you in anything that was doctor related, but you really didn't want to be a doctor. You just said something so you could get back to playing. But here you are stuck because your parents or those around you now expected that outcome and you lived your life feeling like you could not disappoint your family. Your community. You become what they expect and ignore your own desires.

The artist or scientist that is buried deep inside you still wants to emerge. Your dream can still emerge. What would happen if you believed in yourself and changed careers? People do it all the time. Why not you? You can always take classes online or volunteer with an artist or get a scientist as a mentor. You're only limited by how much you limit yourself.

For others, you thought about your dreams many times along the way, but things did not fall in line for you to accomplish them. Your parents were just as invested in you achieving your dreams; they just didn't have the means to nurture them. Even if you were on a path to achieve them, some unexpected thing happened that caused you to have to change course. As some would say, life just happened.

Maybe you couldn't go to school because you had to help out your family financially or help with younger siblings, ailing parents or you simply didn't have the grades to be accepted into college. You may have wanted a job in a particular field. You couldn't find one in your hometown where you wanted to stay, so you just took any job. Before you knew it, 20 years had passed and you settled because you were comfortable and you would leave dreaming to the next generation.

Is it too late for you to do what you always wanted to do? To be who you always wanted to be? You are the only one who has the answer. I have heard of sixty-year-olds that have gotten their high school diplomas and seventy plus year olds that have gotten college degrees, so it's not too late. Dreams don't know your age; they only know that they want to come forth. Your dreams are ageless. Dreams don't get wrinkles, and they don't care if their possessor does or not. Bring them forth. Dreams are infinite. Sometimes without a beginning and definitely without an end. They are just waiting on you to believe in them and nurture them, so they can grow.

You may say, "I wanted to be a teacher and I work at a construction job." You're leaving out that you train new construction workers that are hired. You're teaching. You may not be teaching the way you envisioned it long ago or the way society defines a teacher, but it doesn't mean you are not a teacher. Society norms may not fit your mold. You don't always have to follow the rules. Life processes and direction sometimes dictate that you create your own rules and live by them unapologetically.

The world is full of students, and you were never promised that your students would be college age and below.

You can always accomplish your dreams. The traditional way or the not so traditional way, which is always more adventurous.

If your inner fire is still flickering, ignite it with gasoline. Take a course, volunteer in the area, Google it, go back to school, go to school, get a mentor, read about it. Be about it so you can live a life free of constraint.

You define what success and accomplishment looks like to you.

You have nothing to prove.

You're only limited by how much you limit yourself.

12

SHAME

All of us understood that when we were young, we betta not do anything to shame our parents. They cared about their status and we didn't belong to ourselves. We belonged to our parents. We still did things that they would have had heart palpitations about if they knew. Some of our parents still don't know.

Some of our shame has us trying to prove that we have changed and we engage in that process for the rest of our lives. Trying to regain trust and respect from people; some of whom, we never had it to begin with. They pretend to like us. To be rooting for us. When you publicly fall they allow us to hit the ground. They don't rush to cushion our fall. They watch every inch of our being fall and then join in with the other shamers. "How could you? You were supposed to be saved, to be faithful, to be all this or all that. I knew the real you would show up." One act of misjudgment and instead of working to restore us, they banish us. No wonder it's so hard to feel valuable.

Some of us are feeling shame for something that happened to us or that was said about us. That is false shame, it's not legit. It is not ours to own. Don't let people make your life taboo!

You give shame more power by keeping it silent than if you just called it by name. I'm not even saying that calling the shame by name has to be to another person. The thing about shame is we don't even acknowledge it to ourselves. No one talks to the shamed version of you. The worst part is, not that they won't talk to the shamed version of you. You won't either. She is still there. She's crying, she's apologizing, and she's being ignored. She's been imprisoned in shame for days, weeks, months, years and in some cases decades. It's time to set her free, and you are the one holding the key. Cry, scream, release the shame by calling it by name. Tell the 17-year-old, 30-year-old or whatever age you were when the shame occurred that she is forgiven. Tell her it is not her fault and she can hold her head up high. She can rise. She is worthy.

You are worthy. Not because someone said you are worthy, not because you did enough good to overcome the shame. You are worthy, because you exist.

We cry and mope and settle because we think it is the payment of shame. Speak to your shame out loud so you can hear it. So you can heal. Say I was abused or someone made me do something I did not want to do. Say I don't have to be ashamed. It's not my fault, and it is not my job to protect a specific person. They should feel ashamed, but they don't

because I am bearing their shame. Release your shame, it doesn't belong to you.

Don't let people
make your life taboo!

13

CRITICISM

Jenga is a great game where you have blocks of wood that you build from the ground up. You alternate the stacks until it is as high as it can go. In the end, we know the stacks come tumbling down as we take turns carefully removing the blocks one by one and repositioning them to the top of the stack. As the stack gets close to its demise, each player more carefully removes each block. Sometimes holding their breath as if their breath would aid in the structure's demise. It's unstable, and it is just a matter of which move is the wrong move, which block destabilizes the stack to the point that it all comes tumbling down. When it falls, the person that caused it may say, "Ah man" or "I was going to choose another one". Everyone else usually breaks out in laughter relieved it wasn't them that ended the game.

Imagine standing tall and being strong. As quickly as you were built up, people started tearing you down. Piece by piece until you had no choice but to fall into a pile of despair. Someone figured you would still be able to stand if you were missing just this one piece they took away. Those pieces represent our self-esteem, our confidence, our peace, and our talents. So how do people remove these vital pieces from us and how do we remove them from others? Criticism!

Criticism is not helpful if it is given with the intention of making someone feel dejected.

We go about our business not thinking about all the blocks of our brothers and sisters that we remove
because it's no big deal to us. The person is left, in some cases, devastated because they stepped out and tried something new. They embraced a fear, or they trusted when they usually don't, and it came crashing down for them.

Have you ever been made to feel that you are less than everyone else in the room? How can we reverse the game of Jenga in your life and instead of blocks being removed, they are strengthened and your structure is stronger than it even appears.

In Jenga the goal is to remove blocks that the structure doesn't need to stay upright. You may say, "I'm their friend, I have to tell them they are wrong." There are times that they need to be critiqued. Constructive criticism builds someone up and encourages them in their process.

I remember the very first training I completed with a new job. I believed that training was my destiny. I thought the training went well. At the end the training was evaluated by the participants. I was scared and excited to see the raw truth of my performance. Let me share with you some of those responses:

Customer Service Presentation Evaluation: 06/27/2014

"The presenter was very engaging, and I enjoyed her presentation."

"I really enjoyed the presentation. It reminded me that you have to be professional at all times and learn to remain calm. "

"I felt knowledgeable about Professionalism and Customer Service prior to the event. However, I enjoyed the segment."

"This portion of the training helped me to be more diligent in my services to the clients."

"I feel as Customer Service and Client Services could have been combined with each presenter having 30 minutes each so that more time could be spent on other issues."

"Mrs. Donna Davis provided an excellent presentation on Customer Services. 'It's not about You' so don't take it personal."

"Energetic presenter!"

"Great training. Should be required for all new workers."

"Very Informative"

I was on fire after reading those evaluations. Now let me share with you the response that had me second guessing who I was.

"Presenter needs to be a little less dramatic in her demonstrations. I didn't need a comedy show."

There is a time for harsh criticism, but it should never happen without giving the person hope that they can improve. The above example that almost had me turning away from training could have been stated constructively. The evaluator could have stated that "The presenter was extremely energetic. I felt that the drama took away from what was a great presentation."

Constructive criticism can help us to grow. I learned to be open to it. When I embrace constructive criticism, I don't take it as a personal attack.

I was scared and excited to see the raw truth of my performance.

14

APOLOGY NOT ACCEPTED

Some of us may not know how to effectively apologize. *Psychology Today* lists 5 elements that a sincere apology should contain. They are:

1. A clear "I'm sorry" statement. State what you did. Don't say, "If I did something to offend you, I'm sorry."
2. An expression of regret for what happened. If you can fix it, fix it. If you owe someone money, pay them. If you promised them you would do something, do it. Make it right even if it inconveniences you.
3. An acknowledgement that social norms of expectations were violated. Example: "I know I disappointed you with my words or actions."
4. An empathy statement acknowledging the full impact of our actions on the other person. Example: "I know it may take you a while to trust me again, but I am committed to regaining your trust."
5. A request for forgiveness. Example: "Will you forgive me?"

Apologizing has been difficult from the beginning of time. It is an admittance that we have done something wrong. Our pride, fear of rejection, stubbornness, or the knot in the bottom of our stomachs do not always allow us to be graceful in such a vulnerable moment. Sometimes we don't apologize and the person we have harmed, just wants us to acknowledge that we were wrong.

Even as young children, we found it hard to say "I'm sorry." Our parents would make us apologize for hitting or picking at our siblings. They would have us stand face to face and tell us to tell our offended sister or brother that we were sorry. The most we could muster up, even with a disciplinarian forcing us, is to look at them, behind them, or at the floor and mutter, "Sorry."

All of us have said something and/or done something that we either regretted in the moment or regretted later. There are several outcomes that can happen as a result of our apology.

One outcome could be that both parties come to an understanding about the issue. Forgiveness and/or understanding is achieved.

Another outcome is that the offended party does not accept our apology. Some apologies are not perceived as sincere, and we may not be able to convince the person we harmed that we are sincere no matter how many times we apologize.

We have to come to a place where we view our unaccepted apology as being okay because the person harmed is entitled to feel how they feel due to the extremity of our words or actions. We may not be able to mend those relationships and sometimes that is extremely haunting.

The rejection causes some of us to experience multiple responses including Sulking in self-pity ("Woe is me" attitude) and getting stuck in a particular place and time (every time we see or think about the person, we experience all of the emotions we felt when the incident first occurred). The incident replays over and over again in our mind or we get angry at the person we harmed for not accepting our apology. That anger tends to seep into other aspects of our lives and for some of us, we have allowed it to shape how we see ourselves and how others see us.

So what do we do when we sincerely apologize and it is not accepted? We can't always convince someone that we are sincere even if we are. We have to know that we are sincere. If we sincerely apologize, that means that we regret something that we did.

We shouldn't get upset with the person that refuses to forgive us. That could drive us to a point of trying to prove to them that we are better than what they think we are.

Let that rejection act as a positive motivator to us to do better and to be better so the next person does not experience the same hurt from our words or our actions.

Granted, many of us have probably apologized for the same thing over and over again: last week, last month or even last year.

You are a repeat apology person (RAP). If we are a RAP, nobody wants to hear that because that RAP has no melody and it does not rhyme.

At the point that we become a RAP, we need to figure out the root cause of what brings us back to the point where we would make the same mistake over and over again and deal with the root cause. Only then can we destroy the cycle of being a RAP.

That may mean exploring our feelings when we are being offensive. Is it empowering because someone always made us feel inferior?

We may be set off by certain words or actions, and we may not be able to discover what those are on our own. Accountability partners could be beneficial. Having an accountability partner you allow to check you when you say or do certain things is an asset. Someone you can call when you fall and they firmly with grace pick you up. Every accountability instance helps the words or actions fall away.

Sometimes we have to invest a little more in ourselves so that our greatness can begin or continue to shine. That investment can come in the form of seeking professional help.

Remember, we are not the mistakes we made. We can begin to grow from our experiences.

We can't always change what we did. We do not have to do the same things going forward. We don't want another person to feel that same way about us because of something we do going forward.

We have to come to a place where we view our unaccepted apology as being okay because the person harmed is entitled to feel how they feel.

15

EVERY BROKEN BOND SHOULD NOT BE MENDED

We repair broken things all the time. Our favorite necklace, bicycle chain, even the roof on our house. Those repairs are necessary and desired. It does not matter how many times our roof leaks, we will repair it until we deem it necessary to replace it. The same type of repairing should not be done to things that tend to hold us in bondage, but we sometimes find ourselves doing exactly that. When we finally break away from that toxic friendship or relationship and we are made to feel guilty about it, we reconnect and break away again and reconnect again--continuing a cycle that is destructive to our self-esteem. This pattern makes some of us give up on the idea of ever escaping the situation.

Circumstances can traumatize us to the point we feel like a prisoner in our own skin. It could be a bad relationship or an abusive relationship (physical or mental). Mental abuse, like physical abuse, can come from a significant other, a family member, friends, even acquaintances. You may say at this point that your self-esteem is strong and no one is holding you in mental bondage.

Does someone make you feel inadequate? No matter what you do, it is never enough, so you give more and more of yourself because you want their acceptance. They know you want it and they deny you because it serves their purpose. You find yourself in a cycle that does not need to be broken, it needs to be destroyed. Broken chains can be repaired and we need to stop repairing chains that serve no purpose but to keep us in bondage. Those chains could represent anything that has a negative impact on our lives. Overeating, excessive drinking, fear, low self-esteem, other people's thoughts, words, or actions and the list can go on and on.

Some of us fight and are delivered from some of those things. We break the cycle. The problem is the next time we are faced with a situation that triggers negative behavior, the low self-esteem, the desire to be a people pleaser, the feeling of giving up, the feeling that our good doesn't matter or whatever it is, we lapse and fall into our familiar bad pattern.

You need to be able to think about the person or situation and not have any physical or emotional reaction. This does not mean you forget or become naïve; it means you learn how to deal with the situation in a productive manner so your health and well-being are not affected. How do you get to that point?

I remember being diagnosed with high cholesterol in my mid-thirties. The doctor scared me so much when I was in her office. She asked me what pharmacy I wanted her to call my prescription into because I needed the medicine right then. In a daze, I gave her the information and I got in my car to leave. Focused on getting to the pharmacy as quickly as possible.

On the way to the pharmacy, I began to think about possible options I had that were not discussed with me. My high cholesterol was dietary, not hereditary, so if I adjusted my diet I should be able to affect my cholesterol positively. I did not want to begin taking medication I would probably have to take for the rest of my life at what I considered a young age. I did not go to pick up the medication. I adjusted my diet and stopped eating a lot of fried foods and sweets. A year later, I took a cholesterol test and sent the results to my doctor. When I called to talk to the nurse to ensure the doctor had received my results, the nurse said the doctor said the medicine really worked. I told her I never took the medication and she asked me what I did. I told her I changed my diet and she said "Good for you."

That change lasted for a while, but I eventually found myself dealing with the same issue because I was trying to prove a point to someone with no skin in my game. After I did it, I thought that was enough.

I broke the chain, but I did not destroy the root.

Understand that destroying something that has root in you is a process and a journey. Those roots may be intermingled with your spine, digestive system, in your lungs and twisted around your heart arteries and veins, they may be deep. They grew over time, so be patient with yourself and the process.

Aim for the root. Chopping off the head and leaving the root can leave space for regeneration. You say things like, "I'm trying. I don't know why I keep ending up in this situation because I want out. Maybe this is my destiny." NO! You are willing yourself to stop an action, behavior or thought out of the blue. You try to stop smoking, and you are happy when you go a week, two weeks, two months. Then you relapse, and you are mad because you told yourself you could quit if you wanted to only to find yourself back in the same situation. You did not deal with the root.

What is the root of your bondage? Uncover the root, remove it and be free.

1. Deal with one bondage or chain at a time. Trying to deal with everything at once will discourage you if you don't have the skills to deal with multiple issues at once.
2. Think about how the bondage affects you. Does it cause you to go into a rage, to shut down, to be vindictive? Think about the physical, emotional, and psychological.
3. Lean into those feelings. Allow yourself to feel everything that encompasses.
4. Acknowledge that the feelings you have are real. Don't ignore them or hope they just go away. If you feel angry, speak it out loud.
5. What is the root of that feeling or action? What is it really about? Did something happen at another point in your life that makes you cringe whenever someone says a certain phrase or makes certain gestures? What is it about the person or situation that brings out the negative response in you? Is it someone from your childhood or a close family member that you can't lash out at, so you internalize those feelings and project them onto people that are easier targets?

Destroying something that has root in you is a process and a journey.

16

DON'T LET FEAR BE A FACTOR

The moment you realized that what you feared was really no big deal, you probably couldn't believe it. While experiencing your fear, the adrenaline rush, sweaty palms, accelerated heart rate and the free-flowing tears have to mean that you can't overcome your fear. Whatever brought change to your mind and heart, one day you decided to close your eyes, breathe slowly and take a leap.

Most fear is just a mirage: Something that appears real but is not.

Fear of failure is a mirage because we never aim to fail. When we leap and move forward, we realize the fear is a mirage. Even if we don't achieve what we set out to do, we didn't fail; we just haven't gotten there yet. Or perhaps we used the wrong technique, and we learn something about the journey to our destination.

To fail is to be unsuccessful in achieving one's goal. One way to guarantee failure is to never try. You are successful if you fail 99 times and get up 100 times. Who wants to fail? No one, but everyone does at one point or another.

If the desire is in you, you possess what you need to make your desire a reality. Someone needs the musician, artist, counselor, writer, dancer, motivator in you. Take the leap. Your dreams are important and shouldn't remain just dreams. What one act can you do to make your dream a reality? You are worth the leap. Believe in yourself. Start in your house, your basement, your car, your yard. Get it out of your heart and into the tangible world.

When you get to the point where your fear screams less because the desire to carry out your dream overwhelms the fear—leap! When the fear is still loudest, you might as well leap and take it with you. You will find that fear will abandon you once you're in the air, because you are showing faith. Fear and faith cannot occupy the same space at the same time.

When you press forward despite your fear, you win. Fear doesn't become a factor. Look fear in the face and say, "We are moving forward in this. Come if you want". It won't go; it's a mirage.

How to achieve your dreams without fear as a factor:

- Pick one dream at a time and work on that.
    - When we have multiple things we want to accomplish and we work a little on this and a little on that, nothing gets completed. Everything seems overwhelming and before we know it, a lot of time has passed and we just give up on all of it.
- Break your dream into bite size chunks
    - Organize the steps in order if one must happen before another.
    - Work on one chunk at a time.
    - If you can't work on the items grouped together, work on the independent chunks.
- If money is one of your needed chunks:

    - Stop spending money on something you don't need and spend it on part of your dream. "I was challenged to spend money on my business every time I wanted to buy something I didn't need."
- Whatever you attempt does not have to be perfect. Perfection is an evolutionary process that is always ongoing. You just have to be committed.
- Beginning scale does not matter.

Remember, you can begin with a laptop on your couch. Just begin.

You have to see yourself leaping before you leap in the physical. Don't physically stand if you are laying down mentally. Get up in the Spirit.

How to effectively leap:

1. Stand up. You can't leap if you are not alert or are sitting down. If you are standing, that means you are ready. Stand up physically and in your spirit. You know success is in you; you want it or you wouldn't fear not achieving it. Standing up helps you to:
2. Focus on what you want to accomplish and see yourself successful. Be aware of what you would want to accomplish if fear was not a factor.
3. Position Yourself-In order to leap, you have to bend at the knees, elbows bent at your sides. At this point you have a picture of your destination and you see what your obstacles are that you have to leap over. You muster up all your energy to land when you leap. You have enough wind in your sail to leap over your obstacles, so you pull your arms back and:
4. Leap-How long you remain in the air is up to you. You may have to be like a frog and leap over and over again.

There is something about being in the air. You're not focusing on your fear but your destination.

Take the following weeks to think about what position you are in. What chunk of your dream can you accomplish? It's exciting in the air when fear is not a factor:

I'm still leaping.

Leap and fear will abandon you.

17

OVERCOMING NEGATIVE THOUGHTS

Committing a fault is something all of us have done—either intentionally or unintentionally. It is a fact of life that as long as we remain, we will not get everything right. Isn't that a relief? Didn't it take a load off? We are wrong at many points in our lives, yet we spend an amazing amount of time focusing on all the things we didn't get right or on the things someone else didn't get right.

We focus on our errors to the point that we punish ourselves and the positive things we do are screaming out to us "What about me?" We ignore those cries and give the failures, mistakes, accidents, other's rebuke and all those unintentional errors our center stage.

How do we do that? Let's say you got a job promotion. Here's a conversation you may have with yourself: Yes, I got a job promotion, but I should have gotten it years ago. I'm still not making what I want. I still have to work a part-time job. I shouldn't have waited so long to begin my career. Then you share your promotion with a friend and they say,

"Congratulations! Is that all the money you got? you should have gotten more. I would have asked for more."

What we should be telling ourselves about the job promotion is: Praise God for my job promotion. I knew if I persevered and didn't give up despite all the obstacles that were placed in my way, I would be victorious. I need less today than I did yesterday. I'm pushing for the next promotion, the next job, the next victory because if God did it this time, He will do it again. Thank you, God, for the promotion. I am encouraged.

Sometimes the things we tell ourselves do not encourage us. We speak to encourage others and they may even look to us as a source of inspiration, but we don't extend the same level of encouragement to the person in our lives that needs it most---ourselves.

According to the National Science Foundation, 80% of our thoughts are negative and 95% of our thoughts are repetitive. It's not that we do 80% of things in life wrong, but on average we spend 80% of our thought processes making a mountain out of a molehill.

Examples of negative thoughts:

- Fear Doubt
- Guilt Resentment
- Worry Future possible failures
- Past failures

We need some negative thoughts in our lives, and they can be healthy for us. It's the extent that we take in our negative thoughts that make them unhealthy.

For example, if we are guilty of something, we need to feel guilty; however, we need to do something about the guilt so we can release it.

1. We need to seek forgiveness.
2. Remedy the guilt. Figure out what the solution should be and solve it.
3. Then let it go.

These steps will make guilt and all of your negative thoughts functional and you can move on with the lessons learned. What makes our negative thoughts dysfunctional is that we do something, feel guilty, seek forgiveness, receive forgiveness, correct what we can about the situation and instead of letting it go, we still feel guilty and focus our thoughts on the guilt instead of the solution.

We really need to reprogram our minds. When negative thoughts come up, we need to ask ourselves "What can I do about this?" and then we need to do it and let it go.

You may have to let it go more than a few times because some of our minds always hone in on the negative thoughts and not the solution to the negative thoughts. Understand and accept that the solutions are not always going to turn out rosy.

Stop feeding the negative and start feeding the solution.

In the future, when negative thoughts come that cause you to look down upon yourself, think about what could solve that guilt/fear or whatever the negative thought is and act on it. Once you act on it, let it go and see your authentic self-emerge even more.

We focus on our errors to the point that we punish ourselves and the positive things we do are screaming out to us "What about me?"

18

IRON SHARPENS IRON

Iron sharpening iron can be a painful process, but if it continues and is not interrupted, each iron is strengthened by the process.

Someone that surrounds themselves with people that only agree with them have ego issues and are possibly insecure. We should not surround ourselves solely with people that agree with us or people that will take our sides no matter what we say or do.

I believe in having loyal friends and friends that will not publicly humiliate me when I say or do something, but I expect that friend to pull me aside and hold me accountable. It also helps to give examples of what could have been said or done instead. Why? Because I want to grow. I want to evolve, and I want to transform.

I know what you are thinking: If I feel that way, why can't they call me out in public? Honestly, depending on the situation, a public call out may be necessary. Our purpose should always be to help someone improve: so when, how, and where we do it matters.

Other than for extreme consequences of one's words or

actions, we should approach people privately because the goal is to give them another viewpoint of how what they said or did impacted someone. They may be defensive but not as defensive as if you did it publicly. Make sure you are genuine and have no ulterior motives. Be someone trustworthy and valuable as a friend not a fair weathered friend or bandwagon friend.

Unfortunately, we can't always surmise who is genuine to us or not. Someone who has known us our entire lives could be less genuine than someone we met last year, so we have to be open to other people's opinions.

We should actually seek out ways that we can improve. One way to accomplish that is to ask for feedback from someone you respect. I am very nervous when I call or approach someone whose opinion I respect. I have knots in my stomach and I visibly shake because I know they will tell me the truth: the good, bad and ugly. But I respect them, I want to grow and I know they are in my corner. I am not afraid to ask people to tell you what I did or am doing wrong. I am confident in my abilities and with that confidence comes the knowledge that it doesn't mean I am perfect or do everything right. I always want to be in a perfecting mode—never there, but always on my way.

So, when I am seeking out someone to help sharpen me or when someone approaches me for a sharpening session, the conversation goes one of several ways:

1. They point out something I didn't go far enough into or I lingered too long on.
2. I agree because it felt the same way to me or I share why I did it that way and they may agree.
3. We actually come to a compromise or agree to disagree. We emphasize that it's only our opinion and it goes

without saying that we are going to continue being there supporting, calling out, cheering each other on no matter what!

When you feel like your friendship is not threatened because you have to lovingly and sometimes not so lovingly correct your friend, that's when you know you don't have a friend; you have a true friend. You have a family.

Look among your cheerleaders and find the one who doesn't have a problem fine tuning you and that is the person you take on the journey with you. Nobody will tell you that! They will say to surround yourself with supporters, meaning people that agree with you. Well, having someone to check you is probably one of the most important types of support you need.

We all have said it about someone: Nobody told her she shouldn't wear that or do that with all those people that are around her. Be iron that accepts sharpening from other iron.

Don't be offended because someone told you that you are wrong. Accept that you can and do make mistakes.

The more you are sharpened the more effective you become.

Let your defenses fall and see how you are being sharpened even by the people who behave sharply.

Iron sharpening iron can be a painful process, but if it continues and is not interrupted, each iron is strengthened by the process.

19

ADJUSTING IN THE WRONG DIRECTION

The story goes: If you place a frog in hot water, it feels the water and jumps out. However, if you place the frog in room temperature water and raise the temperature one degree at a time, the frog's body temperature adjusts with the heat and it never realizes that the water is too hot. It succumbs to the heat without ever realizing that the water got 1 degree too hot. So how do we avoid 212-degree F water if we are okay with 211-degree F water?

Don't get used to being at a certain temperature. Sometimes that becomes dangerous as in hypo and hyperthermia. You don't always have to adjust to your environment, have your environment adjust to you.

When we want to try a new adventure or hobby, we get excited about it. We see ourselves doing it in our minds and we prepare to move in that direction. We are full speed ahead and a little nervous, but its excitement mixed with nervousness. We are so laser focused on what this new adventure could mean. We share our desire with someone and they give us a weird look, tell us we are too old, or say something "Not positive" that causes us to have immediate doubt. It may also reinforce the apprehension we had, so we adjust and blow off our adventure as just a thought or agree with our dissenter and tell them they are probably right. We jumped out of the water because of a lack of support from someone we wanted agreement from. They actually turned up the heat or maybe they just turned the heat down. What if it was not an adventure that you were desiring to do that they caused you to adjust your direction about? What if you wanted to learn a new language, give more to a charity, get a certification in an area, change careers, stop being taken advantage of by. family/friends/associates, speak more positively about yourself. I would challenge you to not let anyone cause you to stagnate in your life. Sometimes people cause us to adjust to the right or to the left because someone has mis-calibrated them all their life and the only thing they know is to adjust those around them to their temperature on their dial.

If the calibration is done right, there is nothing wrong with it. Anyone in the food industry will tell you the best way to ensure food is cooked to the proper temperature using a thermometer is to calibrate it daily. Some of us have not been calibrated correctly in years, and we are adjusting to whatever environment we are in. We are used to people saying that we should adjust our sister's crown, but we don't know what a straight crown looks like to them. We need to adjust our own crowns and proudly declare that I am adjusting my own crown.

Even manufacturers know when to adjust prices of products according to the state of the economy. Regardless of the economy, prices usually adjust upward. There may be sales or opportunities to get things at a lower price, but those are usually temporary. Sometimes we allow people to adjust us downward permanently. We give them the power to adjust our worth as they see fit. There are always going to be people that don't believe in you. It is a fact. There is something about you that makes them uneasy. Maybe it is your confidence and they call you arrogant. Maybe it is your passion and they call you angry. Maybe it is your straightforwardness and they call you difficult. So you adjust in the wrong direction. You don't want to cause any trouble or make someone else feel uncomfortable by having to face their imperfections or having to accept that you are smart, bold, and beautiful.

You attempt to lessen your impact or your purpose because so and so does not approve. Do you approve of so and so? Have you ever attempted to get them to adjust? Sometimes this adjusting thing goes in the wrong direction. Don't dim your light, extinguish your fire, or sideline your dreams by moving in the wrong direction. That does not mean that you are loud or always on the center stage; it means that your moves are intentional, whether seen or unseen.

It does not begin with big decisions or moments, but with small, seemingly unimportant moments. If we cannot make decisions when it comes to small things, we may adjust too quickly when it comes to big things.

In the coming weeks, when you feel yourself adjusting to make someone else comfortable and their comfort is at the cost of your discomfort or lack of advancement, swim against that grain and choose you.

You don't always have to adjust to your environment, have your environment adjust to you.

20

MY DESIRE FOR YOU

We go through a lot of emotional issues in life. A lot of them, we don't know what to do with, so we bury them and layer things on top of them because that is easier than facing them. It is easier to put things off than to face them. It may be painful or we don't know how to respond, so we don't.

We may stop being friends with someone, move to a different county or state where few to no one knows who we are. We call that starting over, but we are not leaving the emotional baggage behind; we just pack it up and take it with us. Our bodies may be in a new place, but our souls are trapped somewhere else. We can't eat, we can't sleep, we are nervous and suspicious. We tell those emotions to stay hidden so no one knows that they exist.

We actually talk to them and tell them that they are not going to ruin our lives again, and we can't think about them. We are seen as strong and resilient even by those that cause us pain, but we're not.

That abused young lady, abandoned, poor, mistreated and misunderstood is there beneath all the accomplishments and all the accolades, in the midst of a new life. We see it all the time. People ask us, "Why aren't you happy girl? You did that!!"

We haven't dealt with our inner emotional life so she can rejoice. The good stuff just leaves us believing that we are not enough, we can't accomplish enough and we're not worthy despite what those around us are telling us.

We say, that's not who I am anymore. Have we given her peace? We say I don't think about that anymore. Sometimes that means that those emotions are too much for us to bear. As a result, we create good emotions, surface emotions because we don't want to acknowledge the ones that are intertwined in our soul. We don't want to confront those emotions. But the emotions are there and they deserve to be acknowledged and confronted. If we do not acknowledge and confront those emotions, we can't evict them from our being. Evicting them means they no longer have power over us.

Those emotions shouldn't be able to lie dormant in your soul only to rise up at times to make you feel less than in the midst of when you are being celebrated or when you have achieved something. They do not have the right to make you feel like you have to do more when you've sacrificed so much. Hidden emotions don't have the right to secretly tease you when someone doesn't invite you to something they planned.

You deserve to live your life free. That is my desire for you. That is why I share my traumas and my triumphs. It's why I coach, why I listen and why I work every day to inspire you to action. Your emotions are valid and when people say "You're still dealing with that, you need to get over it," I. understand that those people are dealing with some things that they haven't gotten over. We usually respond to them by saying something like, "No, I'm over it. I was just saying." We do that because they make us feel ashamed for still feeling hurt or angry. We let those feelings go dormant and something happened to trigger them and they found themselves on the surface just to be sent quickly back to the innermost part of our soul.

It is my purpose to help you heal your soul so you can walk fully in God's Spirit.

I do this because it is time for those emotions to be evicted. It doesn't mean you will forget them or that you should forget them. I wouldn't be able to share if I didn't remember how the emotions I developed affected me-- both positively and negatively. But the difference is they don't have power over me, so I am not ashamed or held back or make them lie dormant. I'm facing them, accepting them and evicting them; removing the poison from their bite and I want to do the same for you.

You may not even be aware right now if they are dormant, but know that I am here when they surface. I want you to live your life to its full potential and you are not doing that if you are emotionally bound. Growing up in poverty with low self-esteem, suffering domestic violence and so many other struggles along the way, I had many emotions buried as I made the honor roll, graduated as Salutatorian from high school, went to college as a part of the first generation in my family to do so, graduated college, received job offers, promotions, certifications, master's degree and on and on. I had emotions that were affecting me negatively, and they had me bound despite my accomplishments. They caused me to amplify my failures more.

I deserved to be free. You deserve to be free.

Evict negative emotions because they don't pay rent.

Following are words I wrote when I was 48 years old to my 18-year-old self.

21

I WISH SHE KNEW

I wish she knew her determination and strength would guide her through her toughest challenges and continually propel her forward, not backward.

I wish she knew the faith seed she placed in God while making up songs in her front yard of dirt would grow amazing flowers as those songs turned into ministry.

I wish she knew she would become a minister. She sang out of lack and of vision and what could be and before she knew it, it was.

I wish she knew she was perfect and beautiful just the way she was.

She didn't have to compromise for the first person that said he loved her.

I wish she knew she didn't have to give up on her dreams to make someone else feel valuable. Their value at the expense of her value.

I wish she knew that she didn't have to smile all the time. That she could express her pain. That she could cry and her tears wouldn't fall in vain.

I wish she knew how very much God loves her. That He created her intentionally.

I wish she knew she didn't have to prove that she was worthy of belonging, worthy of love.

I wish she knew she was strong and not weak.

I wish she knew that she was successful. Not because of any grades or awards because she still felt empty with every accolade, perfect attendance, and as salutatorian.

I wish she knew she was successful because she existed.

Her success was never rooted in achievement but in being who she was.

She had nothing to be ashamed of.

I am so glad that now, she knows.

Reflecting on the things we wish she knew is one thing. It is always a good idea to go back and nurture her. Tell her it's okay to let go because no matter what journey you find yourself on, if you never hugged her and told her you love her, she's still there. Waiting as if frozen in time. She is not waiting on the validation of anyone else; she's waiting on your validation so she can be complete and whole. So the pain can stop being current and become a memory.

22

BEYOND THE MIRROR

Poem by Donna Davis

There are silent cracks
We never hear
Invisible cracks
We never see
But slowly over time
They cover the surface like asphalt cracked in the sun
Temporarily mended-cracked-mended-cracked
There's no use, the beauty has faded
Or worse yet, it never was
And you're used to seeing broken versions of your being
Home-broken
Relationships- broken
Workplace- broken
Outlook- broken
But wait, wait. The mirror's wrong
The cracks are just vapors from the morning dew
Made worse by hand wiping- smeared, a clouded hue
It's noon time now
The dew seeps and waters your root

What had you cracked, now strengthens your core
And it does it day after day after day
But you only look when it's morning
Look at noon.

REFERENCES

Benny Hinn, 1990, Good Morning Holy Spirit, T. Nelson Publishers

The Holy Bible, King James Version [KJV]

The Penny Saver, 1995

Guy Winch Ph.D., The Five Ingredients of an Effective Apology,
Psychologytoday.com, November 21, 2013, August 21, 2021

Faith Hope and Psychology, 80% of Thoughts are Negative...95% are
Repetitive, Faithhopeandpsychology.wordpress.com, March 2, 2012, August 21, 2021

Cover and About the Author Photos: The Peak Creative Co.

For booking information go to:
www.donnadavispresents.com

Follow me on Facebook: @donnadavispresents
Follow me on Instagram: donna_davis_presents

Donna Davis is a domestic abuse overcomer. She understands how experiences can shape our self image. She is a wife, mother, and minister from Columbia, SC. She has more than 27 years of experience serving the citizens of South Carolina. She has a bacheolor's degree in Sociology and a master's degree in Human Resource Development (MHRD) from Clemson University. She is certified in mental health first aid, is a Certified Public Manager, has a certification in Kingdom Leadership and in Women's Entrepreneurship from eCornell.

Her experiences and desire to help women walk in their purpose motivated her to create D. W. Davis Consulting, LLC. in 2020. She is a certified life coach and consultant who helps women acknowledge, confront, and evict unhealthy relationships with negative emotions. She does that through presentations, key notes and programs that empower participants to take intentional action so they can live the life they are worthy of. Her mantra is: Evicting negative emotions because they don't pay rent.

www.ingramcontent.com/pod-product-compliance
Lightning Source LLC
Chambersburg PA
CBHW070930080526
44589CB00013B/1463
9781737786801